Crafty Canines

Crafty Canines

Coyotes, Foxes, and Wolves

Phyllis J. Perry

Watts LIBRARY

Franklin Watts
A Division of Grolier Publishing
New York • London • Hong Kong • Sydney
Danbury, Connecticut

For Clare
and all the other readers who are fascinated
by coyotes, foxes, and wolves!

Note to readers: Definitions for words in **bold** can be found in the Glossary at the back of this book.

Photographs ©: Gamma-Liaison: 8, 9 (G. Brad Lewis), 11 (Sam Sargent), 48; Photo Researchers: 16 (Fletcher & Baylis), cover (Tim Davis), 30, 31 (Dan Guravich), 29 (Clem Haagner), 25, 32, 44, 46 (Tom & Pat Leeson), 45 (Jeff Lepore), 34, 35 (Maslowski), 22 (Van Nostrand), 5 left, 19, 52 (Len Rue Jr.), 36, 37 (Helen Williams); Visuals Unlimited: 1 (Gerald & Buff Corsi), 14 (Beth Davidow), 20, 43 (Elizabeth DeLaney), 49, 50 (Ken Lucas), 28 (S. Maslowski), 6 (Steve McCutcheon), 17, 40, 42 (Joe McDonald), 38 (Ron Spomer), 5 right, 12, 13 (Tom Ulrich); Wildlife Collection: 10 (Bob Bennett).

Visit Franklin Watts on the Internet at:
http://publishing.grolier.com

Library of Congress Cataloging-in-Publication Data

Phyllis J. Perry.
    Crafty canines: coyotes, foxes, and wolves / by Phyllis J. Perry.
        p.   cm.— (Watts Library)
    Includes bibliographical references and index.
    Summary: Describes the physical characteristics, behavior, and habitats of some species of wild dogs: coyotes, foxes, and wolves.
    ISBN 0-531-11680-8 (lib. bdg.)   0-531-16422-5 paper back
    1. Coyotes—Juvenile literature. 2. Foxes—Juvenile literature. 3. Wolves—Juvenile literature. [1. Coyotes. 2. Foxes. 3. Wolves.] I. Title. II. Series.
QL737.C22P446   1999
599.77'2—dc21   98-22023
                                                  CIP
                                                  AC

Contents

Two wolves trot
along the Alaskan
tundra.

Chapter One

The Wild Canines

It is morning on the Arctic tundra. The ground is covered with pale green moss and dotted with flowers. These plants are taking advantage of the precious, short summer. A **pack** of wolves trots briskly across the land, legs swinging in a line. The leader's tail flies out behind him like a black banner.

When these wolves awoke several hours ago, they left their underground den, gathered together, and filled the cool, early morning air with their pre-

A herd of caribou roams across an Alaskan plain.

hunting song. Six wolves joined in this full-throated chorus, each baying a different high-pitched note. Their howls were loud enough to be heard several miles away.

Since that time, the wolves have traveled more than 30 miles (48 kilometers). During their journey, they used their

keen sense of smell to track a herd of caribou. Now they are close enough to see the herd. The wolves are ready to launch their attack.

They break into a sprint and dash toward their **prey**. As they chase the caribou, the wolves watch carefully. They are looking for the weakest animal—one that cannot keep up with the rest of the herd. It isn't long before an old caribou grows tired and begins to slow down. This is what the wolf pack has been waiting for. The wolves surround the lone, aging caribou and wait for a signal from their leader.

Suddenly the lead wolf attacks. He runs alongside the caribou, leaps forward, and grips the caribou's shoulder with his strong **canine teeth**. The caribou is thrown off balance and begins to stagger. The lead wolf seizes its victim by the back of the neck and pulls it to the ground. Then all the other wolves join in the attack. The old caribou kicks, but it is too weak to drive off the wolves. It doesn't have a chance against so many hungry **predators**. The wolves quickly make the kill. The lead wolf eats first, and then the others join in. When the wolves have had their fill, they

Quick Caribou

A healthy adult caribou can easily outrun a wolf.

A pack of gray wolves hungrily devours its prey. Wolves may go for 2 weeks between meals.

The Jaws of Death

A wolf's jaws have a crushing power of 1,500 pounds per square inch (105 kilograms per square centimeter). A German shepherd's jaws are only half as strong.

leave. There isn't much meat left, but an arctic fox that has been hiding nearby dines on the scraps.

A Common Ancestor

The hungry wolves that killed the caribou have a lot in common with the arctic fox that ate the leftovers. Both descended from an animal that lived about 35 million years ago. Their ancestor, known as the dawn dog, had a low-slung body, a long tail, and sharp teeth. It lived in trees and probably ate small **mammals** as well as fruit, beetles, and grubs.

Over time, the dawn dog evolved into five different groups of animals. The members of one group died out about 6 million years ago, but members of the other four groups are still with us today. One of these groups includes weasels, minks, otters, and badgers. The second group has only one member—raccoons. The third group, the bears, includes grizzlies, brown bears, black bears, and polar bears. The fourth group is called the canines—the wild dogs.

There are thirty-six **species** of wild dogs. Although each species is different from the others in some ways, they have many things in common. All wild canines have a slender body, a long bushy tail, a narrow muzzle, and highly developed senses of sight, smell, and hearing. They are extremely intelligent, which explains why they are excellent hunters. The group is named

The Most Common Canine

The most common canine in North America may be living in your house. Do you have a pet dog? All dogs belong to the canine family. Thousands of years ago, early humans fed and tamed a few young wolves. Because wolves are social animals that like to live in packs, they bonded quite easily with humans. At first, they were raised to help people hunt, to guard their camps, and to pull their sleds. However, as people tamed and **bred** wolves, they began to change. Over time, the animals became gentler and more affectionate. Eventually, they became the faithful four-legged friends we call dogs.

for the four large canine teeth it uses to kill and tear apart its prey.

Adult canines can travel fast and cover large areas of land in a short period of time. The females produce one **litter** of helpless pups every year. All wild canines, except wild dogs, have five toes on their front paws and four toes on their back

This handsome red fox sports a long, bushy tail. The fox is an intelligent animal that relies on keen sight, smell, and hearing to find prey and avoid enemies.

paws. The fifth front toe, called the **dewclaw**, is on the inside of the foot, above the pad. You may have noticed dewclaws on a pet dog.

This book takes a closer look at the three crafty canines that live in most parts of North America—the coyote, the fox, and the wolf.

Like all coyotes, this one has large pointed ears and a pointed nose.

Chapter Two

The Coyotes

Coyotes are found throughout the United States and Canada. If you live in a rural area, you may have seen a coyote trotting across an open field with its long, bushy tail held low. Coyotes have large, pointed ears, and a pointed nose. The color of their coat varies. In the north, most coyotes are light cream or tan, but in the south, they are much darker.

An average, full-grown male coyote stands about 12 inches (30 cm) high at the shoulder and weighs 20 to 50 pounds (9 to 23 kg). Its body is 32 to 37 inches (81 to 94 centimeters) long, and its tail is 11 to 16 inches (28 to 41 cm) in length. Female coyotes are slightly smaller. Coyotes in southern parts of the United States are often smaller and have less fur than coyotes in Canada and the northern United States.

Crafty Coyotes

In the past few decades, people have cleared large areas of land to make room for housing developments, shopping malls, parking lots, and super-highways. They have drained many wetlands and polluted many lakes. As a result, animal populations are steadily decreasing in many areas. But the coyote has not been as affected as many other wild animals by human activities. It is an amazing survivor.

Although people trap, shoot, and poison coyotes—sometimes killing more than 80,000 in a single year—these intelligent, resourceful animals are now more numerous than ever. While many thrive in rural

These coyotes in Vancouver, British Colombia, Canada are searching for food on a golf course.

areas, some have found ways to live in cities. About 3,000 coyotes live in the city of Los Angeles, California.

Coyote populations are flourishing because these crafty canines know how to catch and eat a wide variety of foods. If one type of food is scarce, they turn to others. As a result, they are less sensitive to **habitat** destruction than many other animals.

Mice, rats, rabbits, hares, gophers, ground squirrels, and chipmunks make up a large part of every coyote's diet, but they also eat young deer, birds and birds' eggs, insects, snakes,

A hungry coyote has caught its dinner— a ruffed grouse.

17

frogs, and fish. They even feed on juniper berries, rose hips, and the fruit of prickly pears. Occasionally, coyotes attack young farm animals, such as lambs and calves. When no other food is available, coyotes eat out of garbage cans and may even kill pets.

When coyotes hunt, they rely on their keen senses of sight, smell, and hearing. Like wolves and other wild canines, coyotes kill with their teeth. They grasp their victim by the throat and suffocate it. Coyotes usually hunt at night, but they may also hunt during the day.

Coyotes usually hunt alone, but sometimes they hunt in pairs or small groups. When coyotes hunt in groups, they work in relays to wear down their prey. One coyote chases an animal at top speed, while the others trot behind at a slower pace. When the first coyote is tired, another speeds up and continues the chase. This goes on until the group catches the prey. If the prey animal is small, the coyotes eat it all. But if it is large, they may store part of it in a hiding place until they get hungry again.

Coyotes sometimes take advantage of the hunting skills of badgers. When a badger hunts, it sniffs out the burrows of ground squirrels and then digs down in search of its prey. Just before the badger is about to snatch its prey, some of the ground squirrels often try to escape through one of the tunnels that lead to the burrow. The watchful coyote pounces on these escaping squirrels when they pop up at the surface. What an easy meal!

The Call of the Wild

Coyotes are famous for their habit of singing at dusk, especially during the fall and winter. They begin with short yips and yaps that eventually turn into long eerie howls. No one knows why coyotes make so much noise. It may be to let their coyote friends know where they are or to tell strange coyotes to stay away.

Raising A Family

Every pack of coyotes has a **territory**—an area of land where it hunts and raises its young. The size of the territory may be anywhere from 40 to 100 square miles (104 to 259 sq. km), depending on the availability of prey.

When a male coyote is ready to have a family, it pairs off with a female. The two coyotes stay together for life. Each year, between late January and March, the coyotes mate, and a litter of 2 to 12 pups is born about 2 months later.

For the first few weeks of life, the pups stay in a den that the parents have dug together. If the parents think their den has been discovered by a predator, they will carry the pups in their mouths to a new den.

These coyote pups are about 5 week old.

At first, the young coyotes drink mother's milk. But, before long, they begin to eat meat that the male brings to the den. He deposits food just outside the den, but usually does not enter. In some cases, pups born during the previous year also help feed the family. After about 3 weeks, the young coyotes leave the den for the first time.

When the pups are old enough, the adult coyotes leave them alone and go out to hunt. Sometimes while the parents are away, an "aunt" baby-sits the pups. When the parents return, they cough up semi-digested food for the pups to eat.

Although coyotes have been known to live more than 12 years in the wild, many are killed before reaching the age of 3. Young coyotes have a number of enemies. A golden eagle is strong enough to kill a young coyote with its talons and fly away with it. Coyote pups may also fall victim to bobcats, wolves, or cougars.

Playful Pups

Sometimes a curious coyote pup tries to play with a rattle-snake. If the snake is provoked, it will bite the pup. In most cases, the snake's venom kills the young coyote.

The fennec fox's enormous ears make it easy to identify.

Chapter Three

The Foxes

Twenty species of foxes live on Earth today. They are found in woodlands, open fields, mountainous areas, and deserts all over the world. Each species is uniquely adapted to survive in its habitat.

Foxes that live in deserts have light-colored fur that reflects sunlight. They also have hair on the bottoms of their feet, so the sand will not burn their foot pads. They lose heat through their enormous ears. Foxes that live in the far north have thick fur that allows them to survive in the bitter cold. During the winter, they curl up and cover their faces with their thick, bushy tails to keep warm.

The table on pages 26–27 lists the physical features of eight different kinds of foxes. The habits and lifestyles of these foxes are described in the rest of the chapter.

The Hunt and the Feast

Like all other wild canines, foxes are good hunters. They have excellent hearing and vision, a keen sense of smell, and strong canine teeth. A fox usually sets off to hunt at sundown when rodents and rabbits are most active. It can see in the darkness because the pupils of its eyes open wide in dim light. (In daylight, the pupils narrow into slits.)

As a fox crisscrosses its territory, it sniffs at the ground and listens carefully. Whenever a male reaches the border of its territory, it marks the edge with several drops of urine and scent from special **glands** under its tail and on the pads of its feet.

A fox can detect a tiny mouse up to 150 feet (45.7 m) away. When it spots prey, the fox straightens its long bushy tail, flattens its ears, and creeps forward silently. At the last moment, it pounces on its victim. To kill an animal, a fox punctures the prey with its long, thin canines, holds on tightly, and shakes the animal, often snapping the spinal cord.

But one small mouse will not satisfy a hungry fox for long. It needs about 16 ounces (454 grams) of food a day to survive. Like coyotes, if a fox makes a large kill, it will sometimes

cover the leftover meat with dirt, leaves, or snow and return the next day.

Since different kinds of foxes live in different habitats, they do not all eat the same types of food. Two-thirds of the red fox's diet is made up of cottontail rabbits, meadow voles, lizards, and insects. In the spring, red foxes also eat young

This red fox has caught an arctic ground squirrel.

25

Comparing Foxes

Fox	Habitat
Red fox	Open fields and woodlands in Asia, Europe, the Middle East, Canada, and throughout the United States
Gray fox	Wooded areas, brush, and rocky terrain in the United States, Mexico, Central America, and northern South America
Swift fox	Open, grassy areas of central United States and southern Canada
Kit fox	Deserts of the southwestern United States, northern Mexico and Baja California
Bat-eared fox	Open grasslands and semideserts of eastern and northern Africa, and from Southern Angola and Zimbabwe to South Africa
Crab-eating fox	Woodlands and savannas of Colombia, Venezuela, Brazil, Guyana, Suriname, eastern Peru, Bolivia, Paraguay, Argentina, and Uruguay
Fennec fox	Deserts of North African and eastern Asia
Arctic fox	Along the coast of Greenland and in the northern sections of Canada, Alaska, Iceland, Scandinavia, and Siberia

Physical Features

Weighs 10 to 15 pounds (4.5 to 6.8 kg); 22 to 25 inches (56 to 64 cm) long; tail 14 to 16 inches (36 to 41 cm) long; long, pointed ears and a narrow, pointed nose; fur is reddish brown on top and white underneath; white on tip of tail; dense undercoat of fur is covered with long, stiff guard hairs

Weighs 5 1/2 to 15 1/2 pounds (2.5 to 7 kg); 19 to 20 inches (48 to 51 cm) long; tail 4 to 11 inches (10 to 28 cm) long; smaller nose and tail than red fox; black and white speckled fur on back and belly, yellowish or rusty-brown hairs on the neck and legs; tail has a black tip; often a black stripe along the spine

Weighs 4 to 5 pounds (1.8 to 2.3 kg); 14 1/2 to 21 inches (37 to 53 cm) long; tail 8 1/2 to 13 1/2 inches (22 to 34 cm) long; buff-colored; dark spot on each side of its snout and the tip of its tail

Weighs 3 to 6 pounds (1.4 to 2.7 kg); 14 1/2 to 20 inches (37 to 51 cm) long; tail 8 1/2 to 12 1/2 inches (22 to 32 cm) long; similar in appearance to the swift fox but paler; large ears

Weighs 6 to 12 pounds (2.7 to 5.4 kg); 22 to 25 inches (56 to 64 cm) long; tail 14 to 16 inches (36 to 41 cm) long; has very large ears; fur is gray-brown or yellowish; legs and the tip of its tail are black

Weighs 13 to 15 1/2 pounds (6 to 7 kg); 23 to 28 inches (58 to 71 cm) long; tail 12 inches (30 cm) long; sides and back are usually pale gray to brown with a yellowish tint, face and front of legs are reddish, underparts are white, and the tips of its ears and back of its legs are black

Smallest fox; weighs about 3 1/2 pounds (1.6 kg); 14 1/2 to 16 inches (37 to 41 cm) long; tail 7 to 12 inches (18 to 30 cm) with a large tuft of blackish hair at the tip; yellow fur that reflects the sunlight and a woolly undercoat that insulates the body against heat and cold; fur on the bottom of its feet protect against hot desert sand; enormous ears

Weighs 7 to 15 pounds (3.2 to 6.8 kg); 17 1/2 to 30 inches (44 to 76 cm) long; tail 10 to 17 inches (25 to 43 cm) long; fur is white to dark, bluish-gray in winter and tawny on the back and yellowish underneath in the summer; thick hair over its pads and claws to keep feet warm; can survive temperatures as low as –80°F (–62°C); ears are shorter and more rounded that those of other foxes

Up a Tree

The gray fox is the only member of the canine family that climbs trees. It can even jump from branch to branch.

quail, pheasants, and grouse. In summer and fall, red foxes feed on fruits and berries, including fallen apples and pears. They also feast on wasp **larvae**, beetles, crickets, and grasshoppers.

Besides mice, squirrels, and rabbits, gray foxes eat spiders, centipedes, scorpions, and other small creatures. They also enjoy cherries, apples, persimmons, grapes, and other kinds of fruit. Like most desert creatures, kit foxes stay in their underground dens most of the day. In the late afternoon and evening, they hunt rabbits, kangaroo rats, mice, lizards, insects, plants, and eggs.

Termites make up most of the diet of bat-eared foxes. Often a group of foxes forages and devours termite nests together. They also eat beetles, grubs, fruits, small rodents, eggs, young birds, and **carrion**. Enemies of the bat-eared fox include leopards, wild dogs, jackals, and hawks.

Crab-eating foxes hunt alone at night. They eat crabs, frogs, fruits, turtle eggs, grasshoppers, lizards, insects, and carrion. Fennec foxes share a series

of interconnecting dens with about ten other foxes. Their large ears amplify the sounds of insects and lizards—their favorite foods.

This bat-eared fox is searching for grubs.

Arctic foxes usually hunt in small groups. Food is often hard to find in the far north, so arctic foxes sometimes follow wolves or polar bears as they search for food. After a polar bear kills and feeds on a seal, it takes a nap. This gives the fox a chance to move in and eat the leftovers.

Athletic Animals

Although foxes normally trot at about 5 miles (8 km) an hour, they can run at a speed of 45 miles (72 km) an hour for a short distance. They can also leap fences 24 inches (61 cm) high, and they can swim well.

An arctic fox digs for food in the snow.

During the winter, the arctic fox's major source of food is lemmings. Sometimes, these foxes even dig under the snow for the lemmings. In spring and summer, arctic foxes eat eggs and young birds, fish, and dead marine mammals that wash ashore. When food is abundant, arctic foxes hide their extra food and return to eat it later.

Raising a Family

A fox's habitat affects its lifestyle in many ways. Just as the climate and terrain influence when a fox hunts and what it eats, they also determine when a fox mates and raises its young. Red foxes mate in winter. When a female is ready to attract a male, she leaves tracks and scent messages for males to follow. Sometimes two male red foxes fight over a female.

After mating, a pair of foxes share their food and prepare a den. Most of the time, foxes find an empty rabbit hole or other burrow and enlarge it. If no burrow is available, they may dig one with several tunnels and openings.

Polar Predators

Polar bears sometimes dig out the den of arctic foxes and eat the pups. Other enemies include wolves, hawks, and snowy owls.

31

Curious and defenseless, these young red fox pups emerge for a look at the world.

When the kits are born—about 49 to 55 days after mating—their bodies are about 6 inches (15 cm) long, and their tails measure about 2 1/2 inches (6.4 cm). A red fox litter may consist of up to ten kits. The newborns have dark, silky skin covered with a coat of brownish fur. For 10 days after the kits are born, the vixen never leaves the den. The dog fox brings her food, and she nurses the kits with mother's milk. During this period, the kits open their blue eyes.

When the red fox kits are about 5 weeks old, they leave their den for the first time. Although the young foxes are now old enough to eat solid food, they are still too young to hunt. Their parents bring them food several times a day. When the red fox kits are about 2 months old, their eyes change from blue to golden brown and their fur turns reddish brown.

By midsummer, the kits have permanent teeth and travel farther from the den each night, following their parents. This can be a dangerous time for young red foxes. They are easy prey for eagles, great horned owls, bears, wolves, coyotes, lynxes, bobcats, and mountain lions. By fall, the survivors are ready to leave their parents.

Gray foxes mate during the winter, too. The young are born about 2 months later. Gray fox adults usually make their dens in abandoned burrows or hollow logs or stumps. Scientists have found their dens as high as 30 feet (9 m) above the ground.

Like the red foxes, a female gray fox may have anywhere from one to ten kits in a single litter. The young foxes nurse for about 6 weeks. During that time, the dog fox catches prey for the vixen and the kits. These foxes often remain underground in their dens during the day.

Swift fox kits are born in litters of three to six in March or early April. They are cared for in the same way as red fox kits. Although adult swift foxes often dig their own dens, they sometimes force a prairie dog or ground squirrel out of its burrow and then enlarge the hole to suit their needs.

Male foxes are called dog foxes, while females are called vixens. Young foxes are known as kits.

What's All that Noise?

Foxes do not howl like coyotes, but they do yap, bark, and growl. They use these noises to keep in touch with mates and to warn other foxes away. Foxes are most vocal during the mating season.

Adult kit foxes stay with their young for more than a year—longer than any other type of fox. During that time, the parents work together to provide the kits with food.

While most foxes do not mate until they are at least a year old, Arctic foxes can mate when they are just 10 months old.

A female kit fox washes one of her pups just outside their den.

If the vixen is healthy and has eaten well, she may have as many as twenty-five kits in a single litter. The young are born in dens between April and July. Arctic foxes build dens in the ground, in rock piles, or beneath debris. They often use the same den year after year.

The Future of Foxes

Although red foxes and gray foxes have been hunted and trapped for centuries, they—like coyotes—continue to thrive. Today, most of the pelts that are used to make furs come from fur farms, so very few wild animals are trapped. This has helped to protect fox populations all over the world.

In the late 1940s, government agents began using a powerful chemical called Compound 1080 to poison foxes. The poison was injected into dead animals that were left as bait for the foxes. By the time this chemical was banned in 1972, the swift fox was almost **extinct** and kit fox populations had suffered huge losses. Although these foxes are still not plentiful, their populations are growing steadily. Because arctic foxes live in such remote areas, human activities have not affected them very much.

A swift fox can be identified by a dark tip on its long, buff-colored tail. These foxes are rare, but their numbers are slowly growing.

A gray wolf is always on the look out for food and danger.

Chapter Four

The Wolves

Two types of wolves live on Earth today: red wolves and gray wolves. Some scientists think the two wolves belong to different species, while others believe that the red wolf is a cross between a coyote and a gray wolf. The behavior of the red wolf is quite different from that of gray wolves and coyotes.

At one time, gray wolves were common in most parts of North America. They were also found throughout most of Europe and Asia. Today, most gray

This gray wolf has a thick coat that is a blend of several colors.

wolves live in Alaska, Canada, Siberia, and along the lower edge of Greenland. A few live in northern Minnesota, western Montana, and Isle Royale National Park in Michigan.

Red wolves were once common in the southeastern United States from Florida northward to the Ohio River and westward as far as central Texas. Until the 1970s, a few red wolves survived in southeastern Texas and in southwestern Louisiana.

Where did all the wolves go? During the 1800s, American settlers began raising flocks of sheep and cattle in areas once inhabited by the animals that wolves normally eat. As a result, wolves killed large numbers of farm animals. To protect their livestock, the ranchers began to hunt the wolves. By the 1930s, most of the wolves in the continental United States were dead.

A Wolf's Life

In the wild, most wolves live 8 or 9 years. In captivity, a wolf may live for 13 to 17 years.

The Wolf's Body

Not all gray wolves are gray, and not all red wolves are red. Arctic wolves, a type of gray wolf, have thick, white coats and live in the far north. Even members of the same wolf pack can be different colors. Some gray wolves are buff or brownish, while others are almost black. Some have dark stripes down their backs. The red wolf has darker fur than the gray wolf. Some are reddish in color, accented with black, while others are gray-brown or cinnamon-brown. The coloring of an individual wolf may change as it ages.

As you learned earlier, all domesticated dogs are thought to be the descendants of gray wolves. So it shouldn't surprise you that the gray wolf looks like a German shepherd, but the wolf

A full-grown male gray wolf looks similar to a German shepherd.

is bigger and shaggier. A gray wolf stands about 26 to 28 inches (66 to 71 cm) tall at the shoulder and measures about 6 feet (2 m) from the tip of its nose to the tip of its tail. Most full-grown male gray wolves weigh 120 to 150 pounds (54 to 68 kg). Females may weigh as little as 65 or 70 pounds (29 to 32 kg). Red wolves are smaller than gray wolves. An adult red wolf usually weighs 44 to 88 pounds (20 to 40 kg). All wolves reach their full size when they are 8 to 10 months old.

The Hunt and the Feast

Wolves have a varied diet. Depending more on smell than on sight, they hunt small prey, such as mice and other rodents. They also hunt large animals, such as caribou, deer, elk, and moose.

Most wolves hunt in large, well-organized packs led by a strong male. This leader, called the **alpha wolf**, may weigh as much as 175 pounds (79 kg). Each wolf has its place in the pack. A wolf of lower rank will give in to a higher-ranking wolf by rolling over on its back, flattening its ears, and putting its tail between its legs.

Most wolves hunt in packs. These wolves are searching for food near Bozeman, Montana.

The Benefits of Being Small

Because red wolves are smaller than gray wolves, they need less food to survive. As a result, their territories are usually smaller than those of gray wolves.

It is not easy for a pack of wolves to find food. They may go up to 2 weeks without making a kill. When they do bring down a large animal, such as a moose, they feast. Each wolf may eat up to 20 pounds (9 kg) of meat in a 24-hour period. If any food is left, the wolves may come back for it later.

A wolf pack has four to fifteen members. Wolves that hunt deer tend to live in smaller packs than wolves that hunt elk or moose. A pack of wolves lives and hunts in a certain territory. Depending on the availability of food, a territory may be as small as 50 square miles (129 sq. km) or as large as 5,000 square miles (13,000 sq. km). Wolves mark their territory by leaving scent-markings on stumps and brush.

Raising a Family

For wolves, the mating season begins in January and lasts until April. Although wolves are old enough to mate when they are about 2 years old, not every wolf mates every year. In most cases, only the alpha male and the alpha female mate.

Female wolves are pregnant for about 63 days. During that time, the wolves prepare a den in a burrow abandoned by another animal, a cave, or a concealed spot. They usually choose a dry spot close to a stream.

In most cases, female gray wolves give birth to five or six pups at a time. The newborns, which weigh about 16 ounces (454 g), usually have slate-colored fur and cannot see or hear. Their blue eyes open when they are between 11 and 15 days old. As the pups get older, their eye color changes to yellow, amber, or brown. For the first 2 months of their lives, young gray wolves stay by their mother's side. They drink mother's

A gray wolf spends part of a summer day with two pups near their den.

Wolf Communication

The gray wolf has a very distinctive howl that can be heard up to 10 miles (16 km) away. Howling is a form of communication used to reunite the pack, to greet other wolves—or just for fun. Wolves also bark, growl, and whine. Pack members often greet one another and show affection with face licks. Wolves use body language, too. It is easy to tell how a wolf is feeling by the way it holds its short, rounded ears and tail.

milk every 4 hours. The female eats food provided by other members of the pack.

Pups bond with the wolves in their pack at a young age. When the pack hunts, an older wolf often stays behind to watch the pups. Young gray wolves are especially vulnerable to predators, such as bears or wolverines.

When a mother wolf returns from a hunting trip, her young lick her jaws. Then she regurgitates—brings up food from her stomach—and feeds them. Other pack members may also feed the pups. Between the ages of 4 and 7 months, gray wolves gain about 8 ounces (227 g) a day. By the time they are 6 months old, the pups weigh 50 to 60 pounds (23 to 27 kg), and they are learning to hunt as part of a pack.

Many gray wolf pups stay with the pack all their lives, but some leave when they are between 10 and 24 months of age. These wolves may find a mate, raise young, and form a new wolf pack. In most cases, they find a territory any-where from 100 to 500 miles (161 to 805 km) away from the original pack.

Wolves: Today and Tomorrow

The Endangered Species Act of 1973 gives the U.S. Secretary of the Interior, working through the U.S. Fish and Wildlife Service, broad powers to prevent the extinction of animals. According to the legislation, an animal is considered "endangered" when its numbers are reduced to a critical level, when its habitat is drastically reduced, or when it may even be extinct but has been seen in the last 50 years. A "threatened" animal is one that is likely to become endangered within the foreseeable future.

Today, gray wolves are considered endangered in all but one of the lower forty-eight states. (In Minnesota, they are considered threatened but not endangered. An estimated 1,000 or more wolves live in the northeastern part of that state.)

In 1995 and 1996, the U.S. Fish and Wildlife Service released 66 Canadian gray wolves into the wilderness of Yellowstone National Park. By 1998, an estimated 150 gray wolves were living in Yellowstone and central Idaho.

While many people agree with the decision to reintroduce gray wolves, others oppose it. The supporters claim that the new wolves are controlling elk herds and the rising coyote population. But critics say the wolves threaten livestock. In December 1997, a federal judge ruled that the gray wolves had been illegally reintroduced because the Fish and Wildlife Service did not grant them full Endangered Species Act protection. The judge ordered the wolves and their offspring to be removed from Yellowstone. This ruling was immediately appealed. At present, the future of these wolves is uncertain.

Red wolves are also included on the Endangered Species List. Most scientists believe that during the 1980s they became extinct in the wild. In the 1970s, however, fourteen red wolves were trapped and taken to breeding centers. By 1992, about 200 red wolves were being raised in captivity.

Secretary of the Interior Bruce Babbitt and other members of the U.S. Fish and Wildlife Service are about to release wolves into the wilderness.

Some of these were reintroduced into the wild. Although not all of them survived, the wolves released in Alligator River National Wildlife Refuge in South Carolina are still alive. The refuge has large populations of rabbits, opossums, muskrats, reptiles, birds, and wild turkeys for the wolves to hunt.

More recently, additional red wolves have been released in Great Smoky Mountains National Park in Tennessee and on four islands off the southeastern coast of the United States. There is no way to know whether these wolves will be able to survive in the wild.

These endangered red wolves have been reintroduced into the wild.

Kit foxes are just one of the crafty canines in danger of extinction.

Chapter Five

Where Do You Stand?

More than half of the world's wild canine species are threatened or endangered. In North America, gray wolves, red wolves, kit foxes, and swift foxes are all on the brink of extinction. There is still hope for these crafty canines if enough people work to protect them.

What can you do? First, you need to understand both sides of the issue. Read

Many wild canines are in danger of extinction, but coyotes are more numerous than ever. Should efforts to kill coyotes continue? Should other wild canines be saved? Where do you stand on these issues?

books, magazine articles, or information on the World Wide Web to find out why some people oppose efforts to save foxes, wolves, and other wild canines. Farmers and ranchers with dead livestock are determined to kill these animals. Once you find out how much potential income these people lose each year, you may agree that wild canines aren't worth saving. Maybe your parents own a farm or ranch. If wolves eat a few of your young cows or sheep, you may not be able to get that new bike you've had your eye on.

On the other hand, conservationists are just as passionate about protecting natural populations and reintroducing captive animals into the wild. They would like wild canines to perform their natural function in the wild—controlling populations of rabbits, deer, and other animals. They believe that these animals have a right to live, and that we have a duty to ensure their survival.

For the most part, lawmakers are caught in the middle. If they vote to protect wild canines, they may not receive the votes of ranchers in the next election. If they vote against measures to save wild canines, people who want to preserve all natural animal populations will vote against them. In the end, efforts to save wild canine populations will not succeed unless people with opposing views can work out a compromise.

Glossary

alpha wolf—the male leader of a wolf pack.

bred—chose particular individuals to mate, so that their young would have particular physical features or behave in a certain way.

canine teeth—long, pointed teeth used for jabbing prey and ripping flesh.

carrion—a dead, and often rotting, animal.

dewclaw—a small claw that no longer serves any practical use.

extinct—no longer in existence.

gland—a cell or group of cells in the skin that releases a liquid substance.

habitat—the special surroundings needed by an animal for its survival.

larva (plural **larvae**)—the first stage of an insect's life.

litter—a group of young born at the same time.

mammal—an animal that has a backbone, feeds its young with mother's milk, and regulates its own body temperature.

pack—the name given to a group of hunting animals such as wild dogs or wolves.

predator—an animal that catches and feeds on other animals.

prey—an animal hunted by other animals.

species—a group of animals that can mate and produce healthy young.

territory—the area in which an animal hunts, breeds, and sleeps.

To Find Out More

Books

Hirsch, Ron. *When the Wolves Return*. New York: Cobblehill Books, 1995.

Pringle, Laurence. *The Controversial Coyote: Predation, Politics, and Ecology*. New York: Harcourt Brace Jovanovich, 1977.

Ryden, Hope. *Your Dog's Wild Cousins*. New York: Dutton, 1994.

Turbak, Gary. *Twilight Hunters: Wolves, Coyotes, and Foxes*. Flagstaff, AZ: Northland Publishing, 1987.

Zeaman, John. *How the Wolf Became the Dog*. Danbury, CT: Franklin Watts, 1998.

Videos

White Wolf. Vestron Video/National Geographic Society, 1988.

Wolf: Predators of the Wild. Time-Life Video Burbank/ Warner Home Video, 1994.

Yellowstone: Realm of the Coyote. National Geographic Video, 1995.

Organizations and Online Sites

Alliance for the Wild Rockies
P.O. Box 8731
Missoula, MT 59807
http://www.wildrockies.org/AWR/
The purpose of this organization is to protect the Northern Rockies bioregion from habitat destruction and deforestation.

Defenders of Wildlife
1101 14th St. NW #1400
Washington, DC 20005
http://www.defenders.org/index.html
This organization is dedicated to the protection of all native wild animals and plants in their natural environment.

Greater Yellowstone Coalition
P.O. Box 1874
Bozeman, MT 59715
http://www.bullitt.org/nrc.htm
This organization works to preserve and protect the Greater
Yellowstone ecosystem.

National Wildlife Federation
8925 Leesburg Pike
Vienna, VA 22184
http://www.nwf.org/
This group works to promote environmental education and to
inspire and assist people to conserve our natural resources.

Sierra Club
730 Polk Street
San Francisco, CA 94109
*http://www.archive.org/pres96/websites-mar/nader/www.sierra-
club.org/html*
This organization promotes conservation of the natural environment by influencing public policy decisions.

A Note
on Sources

In doing research, I think it is important to call upon as many sources as possible. First, I consult with a reference librarian who knows the collection well. Then I read books already written for young readers on my topic. Next, I read standard reference works, such as *The Encyclopedia of Mammals* by David Macdonald, for general information. I narrow my search by consulting more specialized books, such as *Wild Dogs: The Wolves, Coyotes, and Foxes of North America* by Ervin A. Bauer. I seek out firsthand accounts, such as Farley Mowat's *Never Cry Wolf*, Francois Leydet's *The Coyote: Defiant Songdog of the West*, and Peter Steinhart's *The Company of Wolves*. I also study issues-related books like Laurence Pringle's *Controversial Coyote: Predation, Politics, and Ecology*.

When possible, I make firsthand observations by visiting animals in the wild or in zoos. I have been lucky enough to see foxes in Denali National Park in Alaska, near Crater Lake in Oregon, and on Isle Royale National Park in Michigan. Although I also looked for wolves there, I didn't see any. I've observed coyotes in Rocky Mountain National Park in Colorado and in fields not far from my home in Boulder County, Colorado. I keep alert to articles in newspapers and magazines and watch National Geographic videos such as *Yellowstone*, which features coyotes.

—*Phyllis J. Perry*

Index

Numbers in *italics* indicate illustrations.

About the Author

Phyllis J. Perry has worked as an elementary schoolteacher and principal and has written three dozen books for teachers and young people. Her most recent books for Franklin Watts are *Bats: The Amazing Upside-Downers, Crocodilians: Reminders of the Age of Dinosaurs, The Snow Cats, Hide and Seek: Creatures in Camouflage, Armor to Venom: Animal Defenses,* and *The Freshwater Giants: Hippopotamuses, River Dolphins, and Manatees.* She received her doctorate in Curriculum and Instruction from the University of Colorado. Dr. Perry lives with her husband, David, in Boulder, Colorado. In their travels they have often encountered foxes and coyotes, but have not yet come face-to-face with a wolf!